My Teacher

by Michèle Dufresne

pioneer valley educational press

My teacher is reading.

3

My teacher is writing.

On the chalkboard:
```
40 - 9.15
1) Jobs - Attendance
2) Clean Stage, Clean desks Bookbag
                        Spelling
15 - 10.15 -
.15 - 11.30
1.30 -
2.00 -
2.35 -
1.15 -
1.40 - 2
2.00 - 2
2.45 -
H/W
```

On the whiteboard:
① What does friend mean to me?

② How can I be a good friend?

③ Create a scene that shows friendship.

My teacher is singing.

My teacher is counting.

My teacher is drawing.

My teacher is clapping.

My teacher is talking.

I love my teacher.